EMPOWERED MINDSET IN YOU

A Guide to Unlocking Your Full Potential

HAMZA FAGGE AHMAD

Cover design by: Mai Nama Designs
Kano State, Nigeria +2349032351400

This book is dedicated to all Entrepreneurs around the world most especially YOU that is reading this.

CONTENTS

INTRODUCTION

Your thoughts are powerful. They shape your perceptions, influence your emotions, and ultimately determine the course of your life. In this chapter, we embark on a journey to unravel the intricate world of your inner dialogue—a world that holds the key to unlocking your true potential. By understanding and reshaping the way you talk to yourself, you can pave the way for positive transformations and a mindset that empowers you to overcome any challenge.

CHAPTER 1: UNDERSTANDING YOUR INNER DIALOGUE

1.1 The Power Of Self-Talk:

Positive vs. Negative: We explore the impact of positive and negative self-talk on your emotions, behavior, and overall well-being. Real-life examples illustrate how a shift in your inner dialogue can lead to profound changes in your outlook on life.

Identifying Limiting Beliefs: Through introspective exercises, you'll learn to identify and challenge self-limiting beliefs that may be holding you back.

We delve into common cognitive distortions and provide tools to reframe these thoughts into empowering affirmations.

1.2 The Mind-Emotion Connection:

Emotional Intelligence: Understanding the connection between thoughts and emotions is crucial. We explore the concept of emotional intelligence, offering insights into recognizing and managing your emotions for a more balanced and resilient mindset.

Mindfulness Practices: Practical mindfulness exercises guide you in becoming more aware of your thoughts without judgment. Mindfulness is a powerful tool for breaking the cycle of negative thinking and fostering a greater sense of self-awareness.

1.3 Cultivating A Positive Mindset:

Gratitude Practices: Gratitude has the transformative power to shift your focus from what's lacking to what you have. We introduce gratitude practices and exercises to cultivate a positive mindset, fostering a greater sense of abundance in your life.

Affirmations for Empowerment: Crafting personalized affirmations, tailored to your goals and aspirations, becomes a cornerstone in reshaping your inner dialogue. Engaging exercises help you create and integrate affirmations that resonate with your authentic self.

1.4 Case Studies And Personal Stories:

Real-Life Transformations: Throughout the chapter, we share case studies and personal stories of individuals who underwent significant transformations by changing their inner dialogue. These stories serve as inspiration and illustrate the tangible impact of reshaping one's mindset.

1.5 Interactive Exercises:

Journaling Prompts: Journaling prompts encourage self-reflection, helping you gain insights into your current thought patterns and beliefs. These prompts serve as a springboard for personal growth and transformation.

Daily Awareness Practices: Practical exercises for daily awareness guide you in monitoring and adjusting your inner dialogue progressively. Consistent practice is key to developing a positive and empowering mindset over time.

CHAPTER 2: GOAL SETTING AND VISUALIZATION TECHNIQUES

Introduction:

Welcome to the transformative realm of goal setting and visualization. In this chapter, we embark on a journey to define your aspirations and empower you with the tools to turn them into tangible achievements. Through the art of goal setting and the science of visualization, you will discover the power of intention and the impact it can have on shaping your reality.

2.1 The Art Of Effective Goal Setting:

Setting S.M.A.R.T Goals: We delve into the principles of S.M.A.R.T goal setting—Specific, Measurable, Achievable, Relevant, and Time-bound. Learn how to create clear and actionable goals that propel you toward success.

Long-Term vs. Short-Term Goals: Understanding the distinction between long-term and short-term goals allows you to create a comprehensive roadmap for your personal and professional development.

2.2 Visualization Techniques For Manifestation:

The Power of Visualization: Visualization is a potent tool for manifesting your desires. Explore techniques that engage your senses, enabling you to vividly picture your goals and aspirations.

Vision Boards: Create your personalized vision board to visually represent your goals. This hands-on exercise serves as a visual reminder of your aspirations, fostering motivation and focus.

2.3 Affirmations For Goal Achievement:

Alignment with Affirmations: Aligning affirmations with your goals enhances their effectiveness. Craft affirmations that reinforce your belief in achieving your goals and overcoming obstacles.

Daily Affirmation Practices: Integrate daily affirmation practices into your routine to reinforce positive thinking and maintain focus on your goals.

2.4 Case Studies And Success Stories:

Real-Life Examples: Explore case studies and success stories of individuals who achieved their goals through effective goal setting and visualization. These stories illustrate the transformative power of intention and focused visualization.

2.5 Overcoming Obstacles:

Anticipating Challenges: Learn to anticipate and address potential challenges that may arise on your journey. A proactive approach to problem-solving enhances your resilience and commitment to your goals.

Adjusting Goals When Necessary: Understand the importance of flexibility in goal setting. Sometimes, adjusting your goals is a strategic move toward continued progress and growth.

2.6 Interactive Exercises:

Goal-Setting Workbook: Utilize a goal-setting workbook to systematically define your short-term and long-term goals. This tool will guide you through the process of creating actionable steps toward achieving your aspirations.

Guided Visualization Sessions: Engage in guided visualization sessions that align with your goals. These sessions help you tap into the power of your imagination to create a vivid mental image of your success.

CHAPTER 3: OVERCOMING PROCRASTINATION AND BUILDING PRODUCTIVE HABITS

Introduction:

Procrastination often acts as a formidable barrier to personal and professional growth. In this chapter, we unravel the complexities of procrastination and guide you through the process of cultivating productive habits. By understanding the root causes of procrastination and implementing practical strategies for habit-building, you'll gain the tools to overcome inertia and propel yourself toward lasting success.

3.1 The Psychology Of Procrastination:

Understanding Procrastination Patterns: Delve into the psychological factors that contribute to procrastination. Identify personal patterns and triggers that lead to delays in achieving your goals.

Fear of Failure and Perfectionism: Explore how the fear of failure and perfectionism can paralyze your progress. Learn to reframe these fears and adopt a growth mindset that encourages learning from setbacks.

3.2 Strategies To Overcome Procrastination:

Breaking Tasks into Manageable Steps: Discover the power of breaking tasks into smaller, more manageable steps. This approach minimizes overwhelm and makes it easier to initiate and sustain momentum.

Utilizing Time Management Techniques: Explore time management techniques such as the Pomodoro Technique and the Eisenhower Matrix. These tools help you prioritize tasks, manage time effectively, and maintain focus.

3.3 Building Productive Habits:

Identifying Keystone Habits: Learn about keystone habits—small, positive actions that can trigger a chain reaction of positive behavior. Identify keystone habits that align with your goals and aspirations.

The Power of Consistency: Understand the transformative impact of consistent, daily habits. Consistency fosters discipline and resilience, paving the way for lasting change.

3.4 Mindful Practices For Productivity:

Incorporating Mindfulness into Daily Routine: Integrate mindfulness practices into your daily routine to enhance focus and reduce stress. Mindfulness encourages a non-judgmental awareness of the present moment, fostering a positive and proactive mindset.

Mindful Breaks and Reflection: Implement mindful breaks during work or study sessions. These breaks allow for reflection, preventing burnout and enhancing overall productivity.

3.5 Case Studies And Success Stories:

Real-Life Transformations: Explore case studies and success stories of individuals who successfully overcame procrastination and built productive habits. These stories serve as inspiration, illustrating the transformative power of intentional action.

3.6 Interactive Exercises:

Procrastination Journal: Utilize a procrastination journal to track instances of procrastination and identify patterns. This tool facilitates self-awareness and serves as a foundation for targeted interventions.

Habit Tracker: Implement a habit tracker to monitor the consistency of your daily habits. This visual aid provides a tangible representation of your progress and reinforces positive behavior.

CHAPTER 4: CULTIVATING RESILIENCE IN THE FACE OF CHALLENGES

Introduction:

Resilience is the cornerstone of navigating life's challenges with grace and fortitude. In this chapter, we explore the art of cultivating resilience—an essential quality that empowers you to bounce back from setbacks, adapt to change, and emerge stronger in the face of adversity. Through practical strategies, real-life stories, and transformative exercises, you will develop the mental and emotional resilience needed to thrive amidst life's uncertainties.

4.1 Understanding Resilience:

Defining Resilience: Delve into the concept of resilience and its multifaceted nature. Understand that resilience is not merely about enduring hardships but actively engaging in the process of growth and recovery.

The Resilience Spectrum: Explore the spectrum of resilience, ranging from everyday challenges to major life crises. Recognize that building resilience is an ongoing process that evolves with each experience.

4.2 Building Emotional Resilience:

Embracing Emotional Agility: Cultivate emotional resilience by embracing emotional agility—the ability to navigate and understand your emotions effectively. Learn to channel emotions constructively and use them as a source of strength.

Positive Reframing: Discover the power of positive reframing, a technique that involves changing your perspective on challenging situations. By reframing negative experiences, you can extract valuable lessons and opportunities for growth.

4.3 Adapting To Change:

Navigating Life Transitions: Life is filled with transitions, both expected and unexpected. Develop strategies for navigating these transitions with resilience, embracing change as an inherent part of personal growth.

Flexibility and Adaptability: Cultivate flexibility and adaptability in your mindset. The ability to adjust to changing circumstances is a key component of resilience.

4.4 Developing A Growth Mindset:

The Power of a Growth Mindset: Understand the principles of a growth mindset, where challenges are viewed as opportunities for learning and improvement. Embrace a mindset that welcomes challenges and values effort as a path to mastery.

Learning from Setbacks: Explore how setbacks can serve as valuable learning experiences. Develop the capacity to extract lessons from challenges, fostering a resilient and solution-oriented mindset.

4.5 Mind-Body Connection:

Stress Management Techniques: Recognize the interconnectedness of the mind and body in building resilience. Implement stress management techniques such as mindfulness, deep breathing, and physical activity to foster overall well-being.

Self-Care Practices: Prioritize self-care as a means of maintaining emotional and physical health. Establishing self-care routines contributes to sustained resilience in the face of life's demands.

4.6 Case Studies And Success Stories:

Real-Life Resilience: Explore case studies and success stories of individuals who demonstrated remarkable resilience in the face of challenges. These stories serve as inspiration, illustrating the transformative power of cultivating resilience.

4.7 Interactive Exercises:

Resilience Journal: Utilize a resilience journal to reflect on challenging experiences and your emotional responses. This journal serves as a tool for self-discovery and building emotional resilience.

Strengths Inventory: Conduct a strengths inventory to identify your personal strengths and attributes. Recognizing your strengths contributes to a heightened sense of self-efficacy, a key component of resilience.

CHAPTER 5: NURTURING HEALTHY RELATIONSHIPS

Introduction:

Relationships form the tapestry of our lives, influencing our well-being and overall happiness. In this chapter, we explore the art of nurturing healthy relationships—connections that uplift, inspire, and contribute to personal growth. By delving into effective communication, setting boundaries, and fostering empathy, you'll gain insights into cultivating meaningful connections that enhance your journey towards a fulfilling and harmonious life.

5.1 The Impact Of Relationships On Well-Being:

Understanding Connection: Delve into the profound impact of relationships on your emotional and mental well-being. Recognize the reciprocal nature of healthy relationships and their ability to enrich your life.

Quality vs. Quantity: Explore the significance of quality over quantity in relationships. Cultivate a mindful approach to building and maintaining connections that align with your values.

5.2 Effective Communication Strategies:

Active Listening: Master the art of active listening—a fundamental aspect of effective communication. Learn to truly hear and understand others, fostering a deeper connection and mutual respect.

Expressing Yourself Clearly: Develop skills in expressing your thoughts and feelings with clarity and empathy. Effective self-expression is key to creating an open and honest communication environment.

5.3 Setting Healthy Boundaries:

Identifying Personal Limits: Understand the importance of setting and respecting personal boundaries. Explore techniques for identifying and communicating your limits within relationships.

Boundaries in Different Relationships: Recognize that healthy boundaries may vary in different relationships, from personal to professional. Tailor your boundaries to suit the context while maintaining your authenticity.

5.4 Empathy And Understanding:

Cultivating Empathy: Explore the transformative power of empathy in building strong connections. Cultivate the ability to understand and share the feelings of others, deepening your emotional intelligence.

Perspective-Taking: Develop the skill of perspective-taking to see situations from another person's point of view. This fosters empathy and strengthens your capacity for meaningful connections.

5.5 Conflict Resolution:

Navigating Conflicts Constructively: Understand that conflicts are a natural part of relationships. Learn constructive conflict resolution techniques that promote understanding and strengthen relationships.

Effective Communication During Conflict: Explore the importance of maintaining open and respectful communication, even during challenging moments. This contributes to a healthier resolution of conflicts.

5.6 Building Supportive Relationships:

Reciprocity and Mutual Support: Cultivate relationships based on reciprocity and mutual support. Surround yourself with individuals who uplift and inspire, fostering a positive and growth-oriented environment.

Embracing Diversity: Appreciate the richness of diverse perspectives within your relationships. Embracing diversity enhances the depth and breadth of your connections.

5.7 Case Studies And Success Stories:

Real-Life Relationship Dynamics: Explore case studies and success stories that highlight positive relationship dynamics. These stories serve as inspiration, illustrating the transformative power of nurturing healthy connections.

5.8 Interactive Exercises:

Communication Styles Inventory: Utilize a communication styles inventory to identify your predominant communication style. Understanding your style enhances your ability to adapt and connect effectively with others.

Boundary-Setting Reflection: Engage in a boundary-setting reflection exercise to assess and communicate your personal boundaries within various relationships. This tool promotes self-awareness and fosters healthier connections.

cornerstone in navigating challenges on the path to your aspirations, while healthy relationships contribute to your overall sense of well-being. The integration of these concepts forms a comprehensive framework for empowerment.

Ongoing Journey:

Your journey to empowerment is not a destination but a continual process. Embrace the idea that personal growth is a lifelong expedition filled with twists, turns, and moments of profound self-discovery. The tools provided in this book serve as companions on your journey, offering guidance and support as you navigate the complexities of life.

Embracing Challenges As Opportunities:

As you encounter challenges, view them not as obstacles but as opportunities for growth. Your newfound resilience and empowered mindset position you to face adversity with courage and adaptability. Remember that setbacks are stepping stones, and each experience contributes to your evolution.

Gratitude And Celebration:

Take a moment to express gratitude for the progress you've made. Celebrate the victories, both small and large, that mark your journey. Acknowledge the strength you've developed, the habits you've cultivated, and the positive shifts in your mindset. Celebrate your commitment to personal empowerment.

The Empowered Mindset As A Lifestyle:

The empowered mindset is not a fleeting state but a lifestyle—a way of approaching life with intention, positivity, and a belief

CONCLUSION

*Embracing Your Journey
to Empowerment*

As you reach the conclusion of "The Empowered Mindset," you stand at the threshold of profound personal transformation. This journey has been an exploration of the inner workings of your mind, a discovery of your goals and aspirations, a quest to overcome procrastination, a cultivation of resilience, and a deep dive into nurturing meaningful relationships. Now, let's shed more light on the significance of your journey and the empowerment that awaits you.

Reflecting On Your Progress:

Take a moment to reflect on the insights and tools you've acquired throughout this book. Consider the shifts in your mindset, the clarity in your goals, the strategies for overcoming obstacles, and the deepening of your connections with others. Your progress is a testament to your commitment to personal growth and empowerment.

Integration Of Concepts:

Recognize that the concepts explored in each chapter are interconnected. The ability to set and visualize goals intertwines with overcoming procrastination. Resilience becomes a in your own capabilities. As you carry the principles of this book forward, integrate them into your daily routine. Let them shape your decisions, guide your actions, and influence the energy you bring to each moment.

Inspiration For Others:

Your journey serves as inspiration not only to yourself but to those around you. Share your insights and experiences with others, fostering a community of empowerment and growth. Your story has the potential to ignite the spark of transformation in someone else's life.

Final Thoughts:

In concluding "The Empowered Mindset," recognize that the true power lies within you. The tools and wisdom you've gathered are catalysts for unlocking your limitless potential. As you continue your journey, carry with you the knowledge that you have the capacity to shape your reality, overcome challenges, and create a life filled with purpose, fulfillment, and empowerment.

May your empowered mindset guide you towards a future marked by resilience, achievement, and an unwavering belief in the incredible possibilities that await you. Your journey has just begun

ABOUT THE AUTHOR

Hamza Fagge Ahmad

Is an entrepreneur since his childhood started with petty businesses in his hometown at the age of 10 due to his upbringing conditions and succeeded through the year up till now that he succeeds and keeps growing.

He is the founder of a Mai Nama Gifts Shop (packaging, printing and design company in Kano), also the founder of popular Frames Republic and a yoghurt production company Yoghurt Republic among others.